St...
in...
loved international bestsellers include *Intimacy
& Solitude, Forgiveness & Other Acts of Love, The
Universal Heart* and *Choosing Happiness: Life & Soul
Essentials*. She previously combined her writing
life with a private psychotherapy practice and
remains a great optimist about love and our power
to make the small changes that bring big results.
She has been writing the 'Inner Life' column for
Good Weekend magazine since 2001 and is a regular
guest on ABC radio. She gives talks, workshops
and retreats nationally and internationally, lives in
Sydney and is the mother of a son and daughter.

'Intelligent, eloquent and wise' *Metro*

www.stephaniedowrick.com

ALSO BY STEPHANIE DOWRICK

Non-fiction

Creative Journal Writing

Choosing Happiness

Free Thinking

The Universal Heart

Every Day a New Beginning

Daily Acts of Love

Forgiveness & Other Acts of Love

The Intimacy & Solitude Self-Therapy Book

Intimacy & Solitude

Fiction

Running Backwards over Sand

Tasting Salt

Spoken Word

Intimacy & Solitude

Living with Change

The Humane Virtues

The Art of Acceptance

The Universal Heart

Guided Meditations: Grace & Courage

Self-Love

STEPHANIE DOWRICK

the almost-perfect marriage

one-minute
relationship skills

ALLEN&UNWIN

First published in 2007
Copyright © Wise Angels Pty Ltd 2007

Allen & Unwin
83 Alexander Street
Crows Nest NSW 2065
Australia
Phone: (61 2) 8425 0100
Fax: (61 2) 9906 2218
Email: info@allenandunwin.com
Web: www.allenandunwin.com

National Library of Australia
Cataloguing-in-Publication entry:
    Dowrick, Stephanie.
    The almost perfect marriage.
    ISBN 9781741751352.
    1. Interpersonal relations. 2. Love.
    3. Marriage. I. Title.
158.2

Cover and text designed by Cheryl Collins Design
Typeset by Blue Rinse Setting
Author photograph by Monty Coles

Printed in Australia by McPherson's Printing Group

10 9 8 7 6 5 4 3 2 1

For
Gabriel & Aokie
and
Kezia & Sean
with all my love

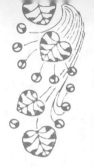

An almost-perfect commitment of love *is* perfect.

The moments you might not have chosen, the habits you've only just discovered, the differences in opinion and experience – these all add depth to your relationship.

The wonderful moments are precious too. *And they can be increased.*

What counts most though is saying 'Yes!' to it all, loving and accepting your partner wholeheartedly, and allowing yourself to be loved and accepted also.

Love is completely natural.

It's the skills that bring love to life that often need to be polished or learned.

You have the power
to lift your partner's
spirits or to dash them.

Take this power seriously.

The choices you make
will profoundly affect
your partner, your
relationship – and
yourself.

Love teaches you to care for others.

It also gives you your best chance to grow up.

It's not age, sexuality, wealth, religion or culture that will determine the success of your relationship.

It is your willingness to discover what love means.

When you fall in love,
you see and experience
the perfection in the
other person.

You also experience your
own best self.

*That vision of perfection
is deeply sacred.*

As life becomes more
complicated, maintain
that vision.

Let it live alongside your
more complex knowledge
of who you both are.

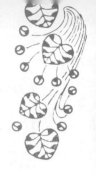

Self-respect and feeling good about yourself live or die on how you treat other people – especially those closest to you.

It's like an unbroken circle: the better you treat other people, *the better you will feel about yourself.*

The better you feel about yourself (and the less obsessed about yourself you are), the easier it will be to behave thoughtfully with others.

Look at one another.

Especially on busy days, take a moment to be truly present.

It is so easy to rush by the partner you adore.

Pausing, looking and connecting, *love comes alive.*

Regard love as the key
reference point for all
your actions.

If you are in any doubt about
the way you are behaving,
ask yourself, 'Is this kind?'

There is no more powerful balm for old wounds than a deeply shared experience of love.

If you have been hurt in the past, trust yourself to get over that.

In this relationship, *assume the best always.*

Build your relationship on confidence as well as love.

If your partner does something that upsets or alarms you, recognise that your own reactions may be getting in the way.

Learning to live lovingly, *use your partner's reactions as a guide.*

Do more of what lifts their spirits.

Stop whatever lowers their spirits.

Could love be that easy?

How do you *receive* loving words or gestures?

If you routinely push them away, joke or belittle them, you diminish yourself and your relationship.

You will also be hurting your partner's feelings.

Practise letting love in. Say, and mean:
'How lovely.'
'Thank you so much.'
'I love you too.'

Mutual trust is crucial
to intimacy.

'I trust that you will do your
best by me – always.'

'You can trust that I will do
my best by you – always.'

Your partner may not always want what you want.

This is a challenge to your agenda and perhaps to your ego.

It need not be a challenge to your relationship.

Don't postpone love.

Express what you feel now, while you have the chance.

The old rules remain golden: never leave the house without an affectionate goodbye; always greet one another lovingly; speak courteously; never go to bed angry; be *grateful*.

Having fun together
is essential.

Check where it comes
in your priorities.

Take charge!

Everything can be survived
when you trust your
commitment. 'We are
in this together.'

Make it easy for your partner to love you.

Easy to love means being good-humoured, interested, appreciative, encouraging, optimistic and forgiving.

Easy to love means being consistently loving, whether or not you 'feel like it'.

Easy to love also means apologising immediately when something does go wrong.

Easy to love means learning from mistakes and moving on.

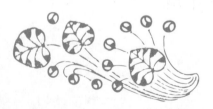

When there is a gap between what you say and how you behave, this will also create distance between you and your partner.

Think, speak and *act* lovingly.

Value consistency.

Good humour may well be the most valuable currency in your relationship.

This means:

- Being reliable in your moods.

- Interpreting events positively.

- Tolerating differences in opinion.

- Keeping an eye on the big picture: 'I love this person'.

- Managing tension and stress.

- Accepting with grace when things don't go your way.

- Assuming that sometimes you will misunderstand one another – and can get over it.

- Doing what's needed *for the sake of someone else*.

- Taking pleasure in your relationship and in one another.

In intimacy, the little things *are* the big things.

Assumptions about gender play a big part in many relationships.

'Women should...'; 'Men always...'

Talk openly about gender and what it means to you.

Discover what stereotypes live inside your own mind.

- Notice when you are slipping into unhelpful generalisations.
- Notice when your partner's expectations feel unrealistic or unfair.

Regard yourselves as two people shaped by gender but not limited by it.

Share out the responsibilities in your lives according to your talents and interests, not your gender.

Whatever you practise
you will become skilled at.

*Practise being a loving
partner.*

Watch other people who
are already doing it well.

Notice what works.
Try that.

Observe what lifts
your partner's spirits.
Do much more of that.

When it comes to love,
think like a poet not
an accountant.

Don't keep a ledger of
who has done what and
what you are owed.

Nor how often you are
right and your partner
is wrong.

Being loving matters
much more than
being right.

A healthy relationship
nourishes you.

It doesn't solve all your
human problems.

Empathy is vital to intimacy.

Empathy doesn't mean
feeling the emotions someone
else is experiencing.

It means understanding and
validating those feelings.
'I am not in your shoes, but
I do care about what you are
experiencing.'

In intimacy you risk
being changed: mind,
body, spirit, heart,
everything.

If you are not happy within yourself, the most loving partner cannot 'make you happy' on a lasting basis.

Take responsibility for your own emotional health and wellbeing.

This will profoundly benefit your partner and your relationship.

Silence those complaints about yourself.

Stop beating yourself up
– privately or publicly.

The way you treat yourself will affect all your relationships, especially the most intimate.

Accept who you are.

Open your eyes to the strengths you can develop and share.

It is extremely tempting to 'dump' your negativity on someone else – especially your loved one.

Dumping doesn't relieve your tension.

Nor can it possibly support your relationship.

Own your own feelings.

Do something about them.

Notice how your moods colour your interpretations.

Trust that when other people seem especially annoying, *you yourself are out of sorts.*

When a change in attitude or behaviour is needed, let love inspire you.

No need to wait until you 'feel like it' to create positive change.

When you behave differently, your emotions will follow.

Share the responsibility for emotional caretaking.

This includes thinking about the other person's wellbeing; remembering what's important to them; making allowances for their vulnerabilities; actively encouraging their strengths.

It means treating one another well, *always*.

The darker side of love?

Often the shadow side of what attracts you is exactly what will drive you crazy.

The 'bold adventurousness' that comes to be seen as irresponsibility.

The 'fun-loving' that demands constant attention.

The 'passion' that becomes obsessiveness.

The 'devotion' that becomes jealousy.

The 'serenity' that can be experienced as passivity.

The 'solidness' that becomes predictability.

The 'brilliance' that's the other side of arrogance.

The 'commitment' that feels controlling.

Accepting your own complexity, it becomes easier to accept the complexity of your partner, and to be far less judgemental and reactive.

Monitor your need
for reassurance.

Learn to reassure yourself.

Remind yourself: 'I am
lovable and loved. *And
I am a loving person.*'

Demanding constant
reassurance feeds your
insecurities.

It undermines your
relationship.

And it's irritating.

Actions matter.

They really do matter more than words.

Behave lovingly.

Speak and act courteously.

Practise kindness.

Bite your tongue when sharp words feel tempting.

Learn to soothe yourself when you are anxious or agitated.

Find creative ways to express your appreciation.

The more 'in love' you are, the more essential it is that you also maintain and value your own identity.

What helps most is:

- Consciously appreciating your partner's individuality as well as your own.

- Resisting all temptation to put one another into a role.

- Communicating enthusiastically.

- Welcoming differences without feeling threatened.

- Enjoying some things separately as well as together.

- Offering your trust unconditionally.

- Monitoring your own emotional needs.

- Taking responsibility for your emotional health and wellbeing.

- *Always* assuming there is more to know.

Check out your unspoken assumptions about what a loving relationship 'ought to' provide.

Is this humanly possible? Or would it need to be an angel?

Keep your attention on what you have and what you can give. *Grow that*.

Accept the power of temperament.

Be clear about your own and your partner's temperaments: easygoing, creative, anxious, defensive, attentive, impulsive, outgoing, risk-taking, high-strung, intense, placid.

Talk about how you see both your strengths and vulnerabilities.

Know what your 'issues' are. (We all have them.)

Making allowances for temperament and vulnerabilities can make tense situations far less personal. ('He's always loud when he's with his friends.' 'She is often tense on the days before she has a big presentation.')

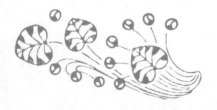

Think about yourself as someone who is fortunate or blessed.

Let your attitudes and choices reflect that.

Do something 'extra' for your partner every day for a month without discussing it or expecting praise or thanks.

You are choosing to express love.

At the end of the month, renew your contract with yourself.

Do you know what your partner regards as most lovable about you?

Doing the same 'dumb' thing repeatedly, *even when it isn't getting you what you want?*

Identify what you do want. ('I want us to feel closer.')

Then ask yourself if what you have been doing could possibly achieve that. ('Fighting, criticising? Maybe not.')

Ask yourself if a change of direction is worth considering.

Support yourself compassionately and with good humour.

Talk about what you want and brainstorm together how to achieve it.

Love is the ultimate 'rescue'.

However, that doesn't mean that in our relationships we should be rushing to rescue or demanding that someone else rescues us.

To avoid rescuing, you need to offer your partner confidence that you trust their resilience and capacity to learn from mistakes.

To avoid being rescued, you need to take responsibility for your own attitudes and actions – and who you are becoming.

At tough moments,
get back to the facts.

You are loving and loved.

Let that crucial awareness
guide how you are
behaving.

Look coolly at the way you treat your friends, family, colleagues – and your partner.

Your partner will always be more, not less, vulnerable to your attitudes and behaviour than anyone else.

Don't expect your partner to make allowances that you would not assume from other people.

Give your partner the very best of yourself. Always.

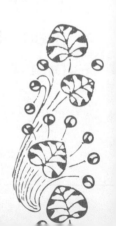

Children, family, friends, colleagues and pets all matter.

But keep your partner *at the centre of your life*.

Let the love you create together benefit all those other relationships.

Love is not love when it isn't generous.

Is home a place of
rest for *both* of you?

Take a careful look at
who is doing what,
and why.

Discover exactly what's
involved in the chores
that you are *not* doing.

Notice:

Who sets the agenda.

Who gives in.

Whose needs and wants take priority.

Whose emotions dominate your time together.

Whose plans can 'never' be changed.

Who decides what's important.

Who 'makes things better'.

Who needs reassurance and who gives it.

Couples can be together for a lifetime without noticing these essential dynamics.

Until you notice, you can't choose.

In a healthy relationship, power is shared between equals.

Differences in age, gender or wealth should not be barriers to a basic belief that *your partner's life, opinions, choices, experiences, actions and decisions are of equal value to your own.*

'I can't live without you,' is not a compliment.

No one should be required to bring meaning to an empty life.

The more secure you feel inwardly, the more secure your relationship can also be.

Inner security is something you must give yourself.

It will absolutely transform what you can then give to other people and receive from them.

Your moods and emotions affect everyone around you, regardless of how powerless you feel.

Take total responsibility for the emotional atmosphere you are creating.

Behave cheerfully and courteously.

Your feelings will follow.

Finding your partner
unbearably annoying?

This is the moment to ask,
'What's going on with me?'

Rather than projecting your
negativity onto someone else,
those bleak moments are
a priceless chance to grow
in insight.

Be aware how dramatically
your own moods determine
whether you are critical
or appreciative.

A guilty conscience can make many people behave aggressively or coldly.

You may make your partner 'wrong' or 'bad' to avoid your own fears, shame or confusion.

This always makes a difficult situation worse.

What clears the air is *facing up to what you have done* – admitting it to your own self.

Then taking charge of your attitude and actions.

Intimacy offers
an extraordinary
opportunity to see the
world through someone
else's eyes.

Take pleasure in your
differences in experience
and outlook, even and
perhaps especially
when those differences
inconvenience or
challenge you.

The world doesn't end at
your front door.

Caring about people beyond
your immediate circle
profoundly affects the
wellbeing of your relationship.

The happiest people are
always the most generous
and inclusive.

If you are leaving one aspect of the relationship entirely to your partner (cooking, paying the bills, keeping the house tidy, thinking about the children's needs), *you are not entitled to complain about how it is done.*

Tasks that other people do can seem trivial.

Tasks that we do ourselves can seem huge.

Be vigilant about what you regard as important *only when it isn't done.*

Think about what your partner routinely does.

Do it for them.

Praise, encourage, admire and validate.

Do this explicitly, lavishly and imaginatively.

This has three great benefits:

• It lets your partner know that you love and appreciate them.

• It reminds *you* of what's wonderful about your partner.

• It is the best possible defence against taking one another for granted.

Never spoil your partner's pleasure.

Learn to be pleased *for their sake.*

You don't feel pleased?

Act pleased. Amazingly soon it will become completely genuine.

Even when your partner has what you want (a new opportunity, admiration, more friends, an easier family, financial success), *be happy for them.*

Being happy *for* one another makes you both more confident.

It also brilliantly supports your relationship.

Deadly arrows are created
by critical words, sour looks
and sulky glances.

Ban them from your home.

'Having problems' is not a problem.

Having problems becomes a problem only when you don't know how to talk, listen and work things out.

When a problem arises, *share the responsibility* for moving forward.

Combine your problem-solving powers.

Sit close together on the same side of the table.

Ask, 'How are *we* going to deal with this?'

Look *together* for solutions or compromises.

Expect win–win.

Regard the strengths that each of you has as a *shared asset* within your relationship.

Brainstorm what they are.

You may be surprised and delighted by what your partner sees that you don't.

Write those strengths down. Acknowledge and validate them.

In tough or complex moments, *remember those strengths*.

Call on them.

It won't always be easy to make decisions jointly, but in a committed relationship big decisions can't be made any other way.

Awareness of everyone involved really helps here.

'What's going to work best for our relationship right now?' is a valid question and often a very clarifying one.

The capacity to
compromise is key
to any successful
relationship.

Essentially it means
not always having to
get your own way.

We almost never ask
the people we love best
how they would like
us to behave.

Do you dare?

Fighting will never give you what you want, because what you are fighting *about* is hardly ever what you are fighting *for.*

When the desire to fight feels irresistible, that's *the worst possible time to engage.*

Go for a walk, take a shower, clean the car: remove yourself from temptation.

Soothe yourself and decide what you want to achieve *before* you raise your voice or your concerns.

Getting through difficult times together gives a depth to your relationship that is truly priceless.

'How can we help each other through this?' is one of the most hopeful and loving questions a couple can ask.

Relationships are dynamic – just like the people in them.

They not only fluctuate day by day, they also have their seasons: intense closeness giving way to a little more distance, then back to greater closeness again.

This doesn't lessen the value of the relationship.

It is never possible to know another person entirely.

Even, and often especially, the person you most dearly love.

Accept your partner's complexity.

They don't always know why they have done something. Or why they hold two conflicting opinions or needs at the same time.

Nor do you.

Shared values strengthen a relationship.

They give you ground to stand on, especially when you can bring them to life.

Talk about why your values matter and what they mean to you.

Lean on them for inspiration and support.

Courage. Kindness. Loyalty. Laughter. Happiness. Good humour. Generosity. Fidelity. Tolerance. Trust. Forgiveness.

Great minds need not think alike.

In healthy relationships merging is never anything but momentary.

Almost none of us know exactly where our boundaries are until we feel intruded upon, pushed around, taken for granted, overlooked, misunderstood or trampled on.

Respect each other's boundaries.

Respect each other's separateness.

Know that no matter how genuinely you are in love, you remain two distinct and individual people.

Take a genuine interest in one another's interests.

Be interesting for one another.

This will benefit your relationship and expand your individual horizons.

Valuing your partner's needs but not your own may be a way of controlling them or feeling wanted.

It is hard to do this without eventually feeling resentful or even self-pitying.

If the words rise to your lips, 'I am doing everything for you,' ask yourself why.

It is a marvellous thing to be a loving partner, but never at the expense of your own integrity.

Surprises light up a relationship.

A foot massage instead of tidying the house. Tickets for a concert bought at the last minute. Developing interests that are new and different. A favourite song played in the bedroom. A note placed in a lunch box or a drawer. A gift sent to the workplace. Home early to cook dinner. Backing down from an argument. A good mood despite a hard day.

When your relationship feels 'flat', don't 'work at it'!

Keep your focus on what's already going well and make time for more of that.

Think about what you admire in other people's relationships. 'Borrow' some skills.

Take time to talk – not about your relationship necessarily, but about whatever will stimulate and engage both of you.

Spend more time with uplifting people. (Enthusiasm is contagious.)

Play more.

Celebrate more.

Create more surprises and treats.

Laugh much more.

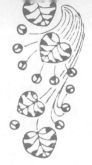

Good talk not only supports a relationship. It saves it.

Over a week or two, listen closely to what you routinely talk about.

Check that it is positive, affirming, *stimulating*. (Is it stimulating to your partner as well as to you?)

Read widely.

Think deeply.

Welcome challenges to your set opinions.

Swap opinions and stories.

Be willing to take one another's advice.

Keep learning.

Your 'messages of love' are not getting through?

Look at your *behaviour* from the perspective of your partner.

Loving intentions are not always obvious.

Make them clear through the way you behave.

When you are tempted to criticise, *stop*.

Even in mid-sentence, *stop*. ('There I go again. I'm sorry.')

Let minor irritations go.

If what concerns you has any real consequence, find a constructive way to talk about it when you are no longer irritated.

If criticising your partner is a way for you to let off steam, express your dissatisfaction with life or your boss, find some other way.

Criticism *always* hurts.

Tension and stress will undermine even the most loving relationship.

Learn how to manage your time and priorities. 'Things are always worse when I'm doing too much.'

Learn how to soothe yourself. 'I can deal with this.'

Avoid turning problems into catastrophes.

Practise solution-focused thinking. 'What's needed here?'

Breathe more deeply and slowly to relax your body and your mind.

Men are less inclined than women to learn how to manage stress. Both sexes need these skills equally.

When your partner is angry or upset, *do not* react aggressively or defensively.

Step back.

Soothe *yourself*.

Engage neutrally and calmly – if you must engage at all – even when you have every right to be irritated.

Wait for a (much) better moment.

This strategy takes considerable self-control. But it powerfully reduces harm.

Love very definitely means sometimes saying 'Sorry'.

If your partner feels hurt and you feel blameless, simply say, 'I am really sorry that you are upset. How can I help?'

Every relationship has its share of unwelcome moments.

Look at such moments *in the context of your lives as a whole.*

If the big picture is pretty good, move right ahead.

If there are a lot of unwelcome moments currently, ask yourselves, 'Why now?' Sometimes something else entirely is getting acted out within the relationship.

Keep a sense of proportion – and humour.

Talk honestly to one another.

Take charge of the emotional climate that each of you is creating.

So easy to talk about how *someone else* is doing too much of this or too little of that.

So much tougher to take charge of what you yourself are doing (or not doing).

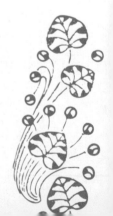

Couples who become happier as the years go by share these characteristics.

- They are genuine friends as well as lovers.

- They are separate individuals – and a couple.

- They focus on strengths not difficulties.

- They can negotiate – and compromise.

- They talk to and about one another positively.

- They can face and resolve conflict.

- They see the relationship as a shared responsibility – and joy.

- They share values and practise them.

- They share dreams and hopes.

- They believe in something greater than themselves.

- They can laugh, talk, play and have fun.

Living alongside someone else necessitates including that person in your thinking.

'How will this affect my partner?' is not a question that comes easily to everyone.

Train yourself to think inclusively.

Habit dulls your senses.

As comforting as your routines
may be, change them sometimes.

Leave your comfort zone behind.

Sleep on the other side of the
bed. Let the driver become the
passenger.

Go out mid-week or to places
you have never been.

Learn a new skill. Play new sports.

Invite friends in unusual
combinations.

Do whatever wakes you up.

Let the leader follow.

And let the follower lead.

It's wonderful to wear
your most comfortable clothes
around the house.

It is also wonderful to see
your partner looking their
best.

And to look your best for
your partner.

Dress up sometimes.

Move.

Get out of the house and
your comfort zone.

Parade a little.

Sex has a special place in an intimate relationship.

Sex can be many things: fun, passionate, healing, soothing, reassuring and, above all, loving.

Just like your relationship,

sex also has its seasons, its variations and its changing moods.

Check out your assumptions
and expectations around sex.

Talk about them.

Talk about what's 'normal' in
your mind and what isn't.

Listen carefully to one another.

Have fun with this.

Get to know one another better.

But also be aware how
vulnerable most people are
around sex – often especially
the people who seem to be most
free.

Timing is crucial in the dance of intimacy.

No matter how urgent something feels to you, *it may be the wrong moment for your partner.*

Learning how and when to express your needs is something that may take years to refine.

What helps most is a willingness to observe the effect of what you are doing on your partner – taking your cues from that, while also trusting that your own internal agenda is spacious and flexible.

Living passionately is another
way of loving passionately.

Fidelity matters.

It keeps your love special.

It maintains the sacredness of your connection.

It deepens trust.

When you are confident that each of you is faithful to the integrity of your relationship, you can go out into the wider world with curiosity, confidence and pleasure.

Sex may be natural but for surprising numbers of people it isn't easy.

Getting help from a therapist who is professional, intelligent and good-humoured is not a sign of weakness.

It demonstrates love.

And positive change can *always* be achieved.

Pressure ruins
spontaneity.

In sex more than
anything, the journey
rather than the arrival
matters.

Many people have sexual scars. Tread carefully.

Be unafraid to ask for what you want sexually.

And very relaxed about whether you get it.

As trust grows, people do become freer.

Though not always in predictable ways.

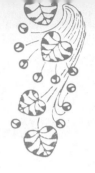

Check out your
different timetables
for lovemaking.

Talk about them.

Find the Middle Way.

And never overlook the
power of surprise.

Cuddle often.

Kiss often.

Hold hands, have a bath or shower together, give massages, cook and garden together, dance and sing, and touch lovingly without always having sex.

Some women like to make love more than some men.

It's not a 'gender thing'. It's a 'person thing'.

Talk about what you both want.

Talk about all the many ways to meet your needs for affection, affirmation and closeness.

Sex is just one among your many expressions of love.

Discover what allows you both to feel most relaxed about it.

Men are generally at their most vulnerable before and during sex.

Women are likely to be at their most vulnerable immediately afterwards.

Taking that into account supports love.

Never ask someone to 'prove' that they love you – especially by doing something that is hurtful or demeaning.

That is childish and manipulative.

It can also be dangerous.

Show that you love them by taking off the pressure.

Romance is a sublime way to express how special each one of you is to the other.

Romance meets our deep longings for acceptance and for soul beauty.

'Behaving romantically' develops your creativity, imagination, tenderness, protectiveness, playfulness – and love.

The big moments emerge from the small. Make them all count.

Find many different ways to say aloud, 'I love you'.

Find many different ways to express, silently, 'I love you'.

Think about one another as a gift: perhaps from God, from the Universe, from life.

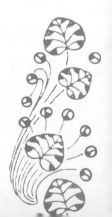

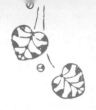

Money is an emotional currency as much as it is a financial one.

Find a system of managing your money that suits you both and is transparent.

Attitudes towards money are shaped in our families of origin.

Often they are lived out rather than consciously understood.

This makes it crucial to *watch your actions more closely than your intentions.*

Talk about money as a way of understanding each other better.

- Discuss what 'enough' means. And what each of you regards as 'essential'.

- Explore attitudes to debt, borrowing, wealth building and 'sharing'.

- Notice which partner is buying the small things that soon add up.

- Never confuse differences in income with differences in personal value or power.

- Do not confuse financial contributions with emotional ones.

- Never use money to threaten, bribe, coerce or manipulate.

- Remember that emotional wealth counts for more than any other kind.

Gender plays a part here, too. Watch for unconscious expectations.

A loving atmosphere is worth
far more than anything that
money can buy.

Most people would rather
be treated with kindness
consistently than showered
with gifts occasionally.

It isn't possible to build a relationship with someone who is never there.

Quality time counts for something only when there is a reasonable quantity of it also.

Beware of 'displaced emotions' – taking out your dark feelings from some other situation on your loved ones.

If you feel stirred up, confused, critical, angry, take charge of those feelings.

Recognise their origin – and why they are disturbing you.

Talk about them honestly.

That will make it much less likely that you will feel the need to act them out.

Take responsibility for your actions no matter how you feel.

Some words carry all kinds of unconscious associations.

Talk about the words 'husband', 'wife', 'partner', 'parent' and 'lover'. They have tremendous power.

Share honestly what these words mean to each of you.

Watch out for the assumptions that you are living out but not aware of.

These conversations may be especially helpful when you feel that what is being asked of you is 'too much' or that you are being given 'too little'.

Never speak about your partner disrespectfully.

It makes no difference if they can't hear you.

In the way you think and speak, you are shaping your capacity for loyalty and for love.

Question the values
and beliefs you grew
up with – especially
about relationships.

Some of them may suit
you, yet until you make
them your own, they
can't benefit you.

Don't live someone
else's life.

Create your own.

Your relationship is not a mini-corporation to be run with maxi-efficiency.

Let it be passionate, creative, soothing, spontaneous, relaxing, uplifting, messy, romantic, precious and unpredictable.

And *what else* ...?

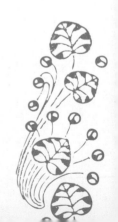

Having children is a privilege and indescribable joy.

It is also taxing, demanding and exhausting.

If your relationship includes children, *support each other in your parenting.*

Talk about what parenting means to each of you.

Focus on what each of you does well. Praise and validate that.

Take it for granted that you are both total amateurs when it comes to raising children.

And that you are both learning as you go.

Every parent needs genuine time off.

This is not a privilege or a favour.

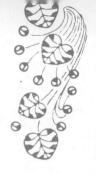

Your children will learn
most about love from
the way you live it.

Sex and housework need regular re-negotiation.

So does parenting.

Who is parenting whom?

Children need parents.

An adult partner needs . . .
an adult partner.

Make time for one another, even and especially when there is 'no time'.

Talk about your own childhoods.
Look at photos. Invite memories.

Sometimes behaviours that seem
mysterious or off-putting have their
origin in the earliest years of your
life.

Seen in context, they may make
greater sense to you as well as to
your partner.

Having talked about them, you may
feel their grip much less intensely.

This is a wonderful way to discover
much more about one another.

Learning more about the child in
another person, you grow in
tenderness as well as love.

Look at your parents' marriages from the perspective of an adult, not a child.

Share stories.

See what you can learn.

Talk about your parents' choices and the consequences of those choices.

Actively choose what you want your own relationship to be.

Friendship matters.

Having a partner who is also your best friend is one of the greatest relationship gifts.

But don't neglect your other friendships. They also bring vitality, depth and reassurance to your life.

When you do not rely on your partner for the impossible 'everything', it becomes much easier to receive and enjoy what you have.

Open your life up to include your partner's friends and family.

Talk about them affectionately and positively.

Value the ways they are different from your own family and friends.

Make them welcome in your home.

Support the time your partner and they spend together.

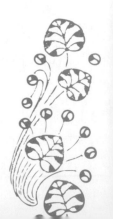

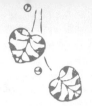

Jealousy sours love.

Regard this like any other
form of anxiety.

Remind yourself of what
you know ('She values our
relationship as much as I do.')

Focus on what's positive.

*Behave as though you were not
jealous*: giving the benefit of the
doubt; not second-guessing;
not accusing; taking for
granted that you can trust and
be trusted.

Without attention, your
jealous habits will fade away.

Listening and being listened to are the twin pillars of intimate communication.

Listen to the sound, pitch, tone and emotions in your own voice and know what they convey.

Listen to what you talk about – and assess honestly how interesting it is.

Listen to the other person, with an open mind and heart.

Take in the emotions that lie beneath what they are saying.

Learn not to interrupt – or push your own agenda.

Talk about listening. And listen.

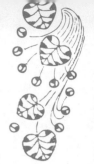

Listen carefully – to yourself.

The minute you hear yourself whining, growling, sneering, barking, shouting, insulting, criticising: STOP!

Even in mid-stream: STOP!

Breathe slowly and soothe yourself.

Like anyone else, your partner will have been repulsed by those behaviours.

And delighted by your capacity to limit them.

When an unkind remark has already emerged, *apologise*.

Never pretend that you couldn't help it.

'Sorry' counts only
when it is backed up
with a definite change
in behaviour.

Careful listening is
essential to intimacy.

No advice.

No putting right.

No interrupting.

No cutting off.

No trivialising.

No clichés.

Just listening.

Listening is a deep form of validation.

'You couldn't/shouldn't have felt that . . .' is a form of trespass that is particularly belittling.

No matter how loving,
your partner cannot read
your mind.

Say out loud whatever is
important.

Good communication isn't limited to words.

Read your partner's body language.

Watch their face, eyes and expressions.

Know what their interests and enthusiasms 'say' about them.

Notice your own body language.

What is your body 'saying' to other people, and especially to your partner?

A loving relationship is profoundly therapeutic – meaning that it can heal old wounds, lift your spirits and help you develop your highest qualities.

Yet it will always be undermined if one person looks to the other to solve life's complexities for them.

If you need a therapist, find one.

You are entitled to say
what you will not accept.

You need to listen to what
your partner won't accept.

Love won't, of itself, make you more insightful.

Love may even make some of your old internal dramas seem more urgent.

Check your fearful interpretations against the reality of your relationship. ('It's very unlikely Tim actually thinks I am ugly when he is constantly telling me how gorgeous I am.')

Give the benefit of the doubt, always.

Be aware of projections. ('The person I am really angry with is not Tim, it's Dad who complained about everything I did.')

Soothe yourself.

Remind yourself that you are now an adult, with insights and coping mechanisms that were not available to you years ago.

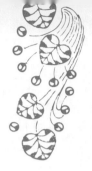

Learn to recognise what you are feeling.

Know how to distinguish one feeling state from another.

Don't leave your partner to second-guess what might be wrong.

Be prepared to speak up and name what's going on.

'I am not depressed. I'm concerned about Mum.'

There is always more than one way to interpret a situation.

No one needs to be wrong.

The person who is open about their feelings doesn't need to act them out.

No blaming others, throwing tantrums, stonewalling, sulking, manipulating, criticising.

Those are the behaviours that kill relationships.

Unhealthy emotional habits
can be broken.

Do something differently
just a few times. *There's your
new habit.*

Act on your power to choose
your best behaviours.

It is easy to react to assumptions as though they are facts ('I know you think I am doing a terrible job with this').

You may be defending yourself against a paper tiger.

Or attacking an enemy who doesn't exist.

Check out those troubling assumptions.

Give yourself as well as your partner the benefit of the doubt.

Welcome being wrong.

Never act out
your complaints
or insecurities
while also saying,
'Nothing's wrong'.

If you must complain, keep it brief.

Speak calmly about how you feel:
'I'm fed-up that you went to check
your emails and I was left to clear the
dishes.'

Don't shout or whine.

Make a positive suggestion that's
also inclusive: 'I feel we should clean up
together or take turns. What do
you think?'

*Don't raise the matter at all when you
are 'itching for a fight' or flooded with
weariness or self-pity.*

Don't jump from this one issue to
global complaining: 'You always leave
everything to me …'

When you have said what needs
saying, move on.

Next time round, you might also
consider leaving the dishes.

Be unafraid to barter.

'How about if you agree to call me when you're going to be late, and I'll certainly agree not to give you a hard time when I …'

Honour your commitments.

Twice each year take a full day to inspire one another about what you want to achieve as a couple or as a family.

Go somewhere relaxing and beautiful.

Take a picnic. Talk about all the areas of your lives. Make some notes and resolutions.

See this as a time to honour your relationship, as well as one another.

Regard your resolutions as a promise.

They will remind you of your strengths.

And they will clarify what's most important to you both.

The almost-perfect couple's exercise.

On your own individual sheets of paper, formulate your vision for yourself and your relationship but *write the sentences as though you have already achieved them.*

'We settle our differences easily.' 'We talk a lot.' 'We feel closest to God when we pray together.' 'We share parenting our children equally.' 'We have the best fun.'

After 20 minutes or so, compare what each of you has written.

Underline the sentences that express much the same intention. Decide which sentences are most important *to you both.*

Write out a fresh sheet with just those sentences on it and put that sheet up where you can see it and be inspired by it.

Keep all the sheets in a folder. Date them. As you repeat this exercise over a number of years they will tell a rich story.

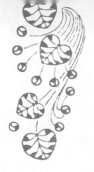

Regard your partner as a soul with whom you are sharing an inner journey as well as an outer life.

Think about what might nourish your partner inwardly and help bring them greater peace and stability.

Acknowledge your connection as sacred.

This doesn't mean solemn or pious.

It does mean precious and love-affirming.

Create a 'relationship altar' somewhere in your home.

Place reminders there of your relationship; photos of key moments; photos of your families and of people who have inspired or supported your relationship; images of places you jointly treasure; a few lines that express something important about how you feel about the relationship and one another.

Keep it fresh. Change things from time to time.

Honour your relationship as a shared creation.

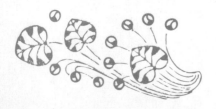

Do things for your partner that they may not even notice.

It frees you from the need to be praised.

The health of your relationship will depend on your individual emotional health.

- If you are tense, stressed or anxious, do something about it.

- Prioritise time for your relationship, family and friends.

- Eat and sleep well.

- Exercise daily. (Do this together as well as separately.)

- Support your intellectual and spiritual growth and make real time for it.

- Limit alcohol or cut it out altogether if you are irritable, tense or reactive.

- Take regular breaks from your paid work.

- Think about your responsibilities to one another as a privilege.

- Regard your life as a gift.

Avoid regret.

If you do something you wish you hadn't, apologise and learn from it.

If you are postponing doing something that matters, *make time*.

Never, ever assume there will be another day, another chance.

Experience yourselves as part of a miraculous universe.

Walk, swim or run together on a regular basis.

Or just sit somewhere quiet and beautiful, holding hands and loving one another.

Grow plants. Watch insects. Listen to the wind or to birds.

Look at the stars. Sleep outdoors. Monitor the phases of the moon.

Losing touch with the natural environment, we also lose touch with ourselves.

The simplest words can
be the most powerful.

'Thank you.'

'I understand.'

'I really appreciate the way . . .'

'How wonderful.'

'I am sorry.'

'I love you.'

You will never achieve what you can't imagine.

Be the partner you dream of.